LIFE
Lessons

WITH MAX LUCADO

BOOK OF
JAMES

PRACTICAL WISDOM

MAX LUCADO

Prepared by

THE LIVINGSTONE CORPORATION

NELSON IMPACT
A Division of Thomas Nelson Publishers
Since 1798

Life Lessons with Max Lucado—Book of James

Copyright © 2006, Nelson Impact. All rights reserved. No portion of this book may be reproduced, stored in a retrieval system, or transmitted in any form or by any means—electronic, mechanical, photocopy, recording, or any other—except for brief quotations in printed reviews, without the prior permission of the publisher.

Published by Nelson Impact, a Division of Thomas Nelson, Inc., P.O. Box 141000, Nashville, Tennessee 37214.

Produced with the assistance of the Livingstone Corporation (www.livingstonecorp.com). Project staff include Jake Barton, Joel Bartlett, Andy Culbertson, and Mary Horner Collins. Editor: Neil Wilson

Scripture quotations marked "NCV™" are taken from the New Century Version®. Copyright © 2005 by Thomas Nelson, Inc. Used by permission. All rights reserved.

Scripture quotations marked "NKJV™" are taken from the New King James Version®. Copyright © 1982 by Thomas Nelson, Inc. Used by permission. All rights reserved.

Scripture quotations marked (KJV) are taken from *The Holy Bible,* King James Version.

Scripture quotations marked (NASB) are taken from the New American Standard Bible® Copyright © 1960, 1962, 1963, 1968, 1971, 1972, 1973, 1975, 1977, 1995 by The Lockman Foundation. Used by permission.

Scripture quotations marked (NIV) are taken from the New International Version. Copyright © 1973, 1978, 1984, International Bible Society. Used by permission of Zondervan Bible Publishers. All rights reserved.

Scripture quotations marked (TLB) are taken from *The Living Bible,* copyright © 1971. Used by permission of Tyndale House Publishers, Inc., P.O. Box 80, Wheaton, Illinois 60189.

Material for the "Inspiration" sections taken from the following books:

The Applause of Heaven. Copyright © 1990, 1996, 1999 by Max Lucado. W Publishing Group, a Division of Thomas Nelson, Inc., Nashville, Tennessee.

The Great House of God. Copyright © 1997 by Max Lucado. W Publishing Group, a Division of Thomas Nelson, Inc., Nashville, Tennessee.

It's Not About Me. Copyright © 2004 by Max Lucado. Integrity Publishers, Brentwood, Tennessee.

Just Like Jesus. Copyright © 1998 by Max Lucado. W Publishing Group, a Division of Thomas Nelson, Inc., Nashville, Tennessee.

Just Like Jesus. Copyright © 2003 by Max Lucado. W Publishing Group, a Division of Thomas Nelson, Inc., Nashville, Tennessee.

A Love Worth Giving. Copyright © 2002 by Max Lucado. W Publishing Group, a Division of Thomas Nelson, Inc., Inc., Nashville, Tennessee.

Next Door Savior. Copyright © 2003 by Max Lucado. W Publishing Group, a Division of Thomas Nelson, Inc., Nashville, Tennessee.

Rich Christians in an Age of Hunger. Copyright © 1990 by Ronald Sider. W Publishing Group, a Division of Thomas Nelson, Inc., Nashville, Tennessee.

Shaped by God (previously published as *On the Anvil*). Copyright © 2001 by Max Lucado. Tyndale House Publishers, Wheaton, Illinois.

Traveling Light. Copyright © 2001 by Max Lucado. W Publishing Group, a Division of Thomas Nelson, Inc., Nashville, Tennessee.

When Christ Comes. Copyright © 1999 by Max Lucado. W Publishing Group, a Division of Thomas Nelson, Inc., Nashville, Tennessee.

Cover Art and Interior Design by Kirk Luttrell of the Livingstone Corporation

Interior Composition by Rachel Hawkins of the Livingstone Corporation

ISBN-13: 978-1-4185-0956-9

Printed in the United States of America.

LIFE *Lessons*

WITH MAX LUCADO

CONTENTS

HOW TO STUDY THE BIBLE

This is a peculiar book you are holding. Words crafted in another language. Deeds done in a distant era. Events recorded in a far-off land. Counsel offered to a foreign people. This is a peculiar book.

It's surprising that anyone reads it. It's too old. Some of its writings date back five thousand years. It's too bizarre. The book speaks of incredible floods, fires, earthquakes, and people with supernatural abilities. It's too radical. The Bible calls for undying devotion to a carpenter who called himself God's Son.

Logic says this book shouldn't survive. Too old, too bizarre, too radical.

The Bible has been banned, burned, scoffed, and ridiculed. Scholars have mocked it as foolish. Kings have branded it as illegal. A thousand times over the grave has been dug and the dirge has begun, but somehow the Bible never stays in the grave. Not only has it survived; it has thrived. It is the single most popular book in all of history. It has been the best-selling book in the world for years!

There is no way on earth to explain it. Which perhaps is the only explanation. The answer? The Bible's durability is not found on earth; it is found in heaven. For the millions who have tested its claims and claimed its promises, there is but one answer: the Bible is God's book and God's voice.

As you read it, you would be wise to give some thought to two questions. What is the purpose of the Bible? and How do I study the Bible? Time spent reflecting on these two issues will greatly enhance your Bible study.

What is the purpose of the Bible?

Let the Bible itself answer that question.

Since you were a child you have known the Holy Scriptures which are able to make you wise. And that wisdom leads to salvation through faith in Christ Jesus. (2 Tim. 3:15 NCV)

The purpose of the Bible? Salvation. God's highest passion is to get his children home. His book, the Bible, describes his plan of salvation. The purpose of the Bible is to proclaim God's plan and passion to save his children.

That is the reason this book has endured through the centuries. It dares to tackle the toughest questions about life: Where do I go after I die? Is there a God? What do I do with my fears? The Bible offers answers to these crucial questions. It is the treasure map that leads us to God's highest treasure, eternal life.

But how do we use the Bible? Countless copies of Scripture sit unread on bookshelves and nightstands simply because people don't know how to read it. What can we do to make the Bible real in our lives?

The clearest answer is found in the words of Jesus. He promised:

Ask, and God will give to you. Search, and you will find. Knock, and the door will open for you. (Matt. 7:7 NCV)

The first step in understanding the Bible is asking God to help us. We should read prayerfully. If anyone understands God's Word, it is because of God and not the reader.

But the Helper will teach you everything and will cause you to remember all that I told you. The Helper is the Holy Spirit whom the Father will send in my name. (John 14:26 NCV)

Before reading the Bible, pray. Invite God to speak to you. Don't go to Scripture looking for your idea; go searching for his.

Not only should we read the Bible prayerfully, we should read it carefully. *Search and you will find* is the pledge. The Bible is not a newspaper to be skimmed but rather a mine to be quarried.

Search for it like silver, and hunt for it like hidden treasure. Then you will understand respect for the LORD, and you will find that you know God. (Prov. 2:4–5 NCV)

Any worthy find requires effort. The Bible is no exception. To understand the Bible you don't have to be brilliant, but you must be willing to roll up your sleeves and search.

Be a worker who is not ashamed and who uses the true teaching in the right way. (2 Tim. 2:15 NCV)

Here's a practical point. Study the Bible a bit at a time. Hunger is not satisfied by eating twenty-one meals in one sitting once a week. The body needs a steady diet to remain strong. So does the soul. When God sent food to his people in the wilderness, he didn't provide loaves already made. Instead, he sent them manna in the shape of *"thin flakes like frost . . . on the desert ground"* (Ex. 16:14 NCV).

God gave manna in limited portions. God sends spiritual food the same way. He opens the heavens with just enough nutrients for today's hunger. He provides *"a command here, a command there. A rule here, a rule there. A little lesson here, a little lesson there"* (Isa. 28:10 NCV).

Don't be discouraged if your reading reaps a small harvest. Some days a lesser portion is all that is needed. What is important is to search every day for that day's message. A steady diet of God's Word over a lifetime builds a healthy soul and mind.

A little girl returned from her first day at school. Her mom asked, "Did you learn anything?"

"Apparently not enough," the girl responded, "I have to go back tomorrow and the next day and the next . . ."

Such is the case with learning. And such is the case with Bible study. Understanding comes little by little over a lifetime.

There is a third step in understanding the Bible. After the asking and seeking comes the knocking. After you ask and search, then knock.

Knock, and the door will open for you. (Matt. 7:7 NCV)

To knock is to stand at God's door. To make yourself available. To climb the steps, cross the porch, stand at the doorway, and volunteer. Knocking goes beyond the realm of thinking and into the realm of acting.

To knock is to ask, What can I do? How can I obey? Where can I go?

It's one thing to know what to do. It's another to do it. But for those who do it, those who choose to obey, a special reward awaits them.

The truly happy are those who carefully study God's perfect law that makes people free, and they continue to study it. They do not forget what they heard, but they obey what God's teaching says. Those who do this will be made happy. (James 1:25 NCV)

What a promise. Happiness comes to those who do what they read! It's the same with medicine. If you only read the label but ignore the pills, it won't help. It's the same with food. If you only read the recipe but never cook, you won't be fed. And it's the same with the Bible. If you only read the words but never obey, you'll never know the joy God has promised.

Ask. Search. Knock. Simple, isn't it? Why don't you give it a try? If you do, you'll see why you are holding the most remarkable book in history.

INTRODUCTION TO THE BOOK OF JAMES

Here is a story James would have liked.

Francis of Assisi once invited an apprentice to go with him to a nearby village to preach. The young monk quickly agreed, seizing an opportunity to hear his teacher speak. When they arrived in the village, Francis began to visit with the people.

First he stopped in on the butcher. Next a visit with the cobbler. Then a short walk to the home of a woman who'd recently buried her husband. After that a stop at the school to chat with the teacher. This continued throughout the morning. After some time, Francis told his disciple that it was time to return to the abbey.

The student didn't understand. "But we came to preach," he reminded. "We haven't preached a sermon."

"Haven't we?" questioned the elder. "People have watched us, listened to us, responded to us. Every word we have spoken, every deed we have done has been a sermon. We have preached all morning."

James would have liked that. As far as he was concerned, Christianity was more action on Monday than worship on Sunday. "My brothers and sisters, if people say they have faith, but do nothing, their faith is worth nothing. Can faith like that save them?" (2:14 NCV).

His message is bare-knuckled; his style is bare boned. Talk is cheap, he argues. Service is invaluable.

It's not that works save the Christian, but that works mark the Christian. In James's book of logic, it only makes sense that we who have been given much should give much. Not just with words. But with our lives.

Or as St. Francis is noted as saying, "Preach without ceasing. If you must, use words."

James would have liked that too.

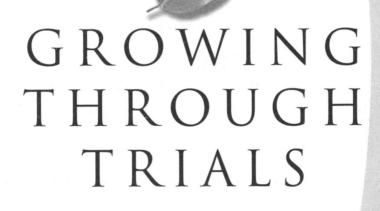

LESSON ONE

GROWING
THROUGH
TRIALS

MAX
LUCADO

REFLECTION

The book of James deals with the practical side of faith, which means trusting God even in hard times. Think about the way you have responded to a recent problem or difficulty in your life. How would you describe your general attitude during this time? What does your response to this situation reveal about your view of God?

SITUATION

Like many of the early church leaders, James served under a constant threat of persecution and violence. Both the Roman Empire and the Jewish religious leaders had reasons to persecute as many Christians as possible. To the former, Christians were troublemakers; to the latter, they were blasphemers. James wrote to his brothers and sisters about the benefits that could result from hardship and the importance of living genuine lives of faith.

OBSERVATION

Read James 1:1–11 from the NCV or the NKJV.

NCV

¹From James, a servant of God and of the Lord Jesus Christ.

To all of God's people who are scattered everywhere in the world:

Greetings.

²My brothers and sisters, when you have many kinds of troubles, you should be full of joy, ³because you know that these troubles test your faith, and this will give you patience. ⁴Let your patience show itself perfectly in what you do. Then you will be perfect and complete and will have everything you need. ⁵But if any of you needs wisdom, you should ask God for it. He is generous and enjoys giving to all people, so he will give you wisdom. ⁶But when you ask God, you must believe and not doubt. Anyone who doubts is like a wave in the sea, blown up and down by the wind. ⁷⁻⁸Such doubters are thinking two different things at the same time, and they cannot decide about anything they do. They should not think they will receive anything from the Lord.

⁹Believers who are poor should be proud, because God has made them spiritually rich. ¹⁰Those who are rich should be proud, because God has shown them that they are spiritually poor. The rich will die like a wild flower in the grass. ¹¹The sun rises with burning heat and dries up the plants. The flower falls off, and its beauty is gone. In the same way the rich will die while they are still taking care of business.

NKJV

¹James, a bondservant of God and of the Lord Jesus Christ,

To the twelve tribes which are scattered abroad:

Greetings.

²My brethren, count it all joy when you fall into various trials, ³knowing that the testing of your faith produces patience. ⁴But let patience have its perfect work, that you may be perfect and complete, lacking nothing. ⁵If any of you lacks wisdom, let him ask of God, who gives to all liberally and without reproach, and it will be given to him. ⁶But let him ask in faith, with no doubting, for he who doubts is like a wave of the sea driven and tossed by the wind. ⁷For let not that man suppose that he will receive anything from the Lord; ⁸he is a double-minded man, unstable in all his ways.

⁹Let the lowly brother glory in his exaltation, ¹⁰but the rich in his humiliation, because as a flower of the field he will pass away. ¹¹For no sooner has the sun risen with a burning heat than it withers the grass; its flower falls, and its beautiful appearance perishes. So the rich man also will fade away in his pursuits.

EXPLORATION

1. How does Scripture encourage people to respond to trials? Why?

2. How has God brought good into your life through trials?

3. How can a person gain wisdom to deal with problems?

4. Why does God want us to ask for his help without doubting?

5. Who should not expect to receive anything from God? Why?

INSPIRATION

When a potter bakes a pot, he checks its solidity by pulling it out of the oven and thumping it. If it "sings," it's ready. If it "thuds," it's placed back in the oven. The character of a person is also checked by thumping.

Been thumped lately?

Late-night phone calls. Grouchy teacher. Grumpy moms. Burnt meals. Flat tires. "You've got to be kidding" deadlines. Those are thumps. Thumps are those irritating inconveniences that trigger the worst in us. They catch us off guard. Flat-footed. They aren't big enough to be crises, but if you get enough of them, watch out! Traffic jams. Long lines. Empty mailboxes. Dirty clothes on the floor . . . *Thump. Thump. Thump.* How do I respond? Do I sing? Or do I thud? Jesus said that out of the nature of the heart a man speaks (Luke 6:45). There's nothing like a good thump to reveal the nature of a heart. The true character of a person is seen not in momentary heroics, but in the thump-packed humdrum of day-to-day living. (From *Shaped by God* by Max Lucado)

REACTION

6. How have life's "thumps" challenged you to seek God?

7. How has your relationship with God changed as you have gone through trials and difficulties?

8. In what ways does this passage relate to your present problems and frustrations?

9. How do you usually respond to life's difficulties?

10. How can you find joy in your troubles?

11. Describe a time when God's wisdom helped you through a problem.

LIFE LESSONS

Many of us have contingency plans *if* things go wrong. In truth, we need a plan for *when* things go bad. If we assume that life is trouble-free, we will have to deal with constant disappointment. If we realize that life involves a mixture of troubles and blessings, we will have better reason to plan with hardships in mind. Trouble may not be here at this minute, but it's coming. James helps us see that God allows even trouble for our good. He doesn't want us to worry about why troubles come; he wants us to prepare and trust God when troubles do come.

DEVOTION

Father, we come to you just as we are, struggling to cope with the trials of life. We're grateful that you never turn your back on us. You promise to give us the wisdom and strength we need to face each day. Continue to test us until our character shines and brings glory to you.

For more Bible passages on growing through trials, see Romans 5:3–4; 2 Corinthians 4:17; 6:4; 2 Thessalonians 1:4; 1 Peter 1:5–7; 4:12–14.

To complete the book of James during this twelve-part study, read James 1:1–11.

JOURNALING

How can I grow closer to God through trials I am facing now?

LESSON TWO

ENDURING
TEMPTATION

MAX
LUCADO

REFLECTION

One of the classic hymns of the church is entitled "Count Your Blessings." It highlights our tendency to tally our temptations and count our complaints rather than counting our blessings. Take two minutes right now and compile as long a list as you can of all the items and people you consider as God's blessings in your life. In what ways have you received good gifts from God?

SITUATION

Shifting from his opening words of encouragement based on joy, James moved to another source of encouragement—God's good gifts and blessings. We will face temptations, James said. Our own evil desires will tempt us to sin. But a follower of Jesus has plenty of reasons for joyful living. God is consistently working for our good.

OBSERVATION

Read James 1:12–18 from the NCV or the NKJV.

NCV

¹²When people are tempted and still continue strong, they should be happy. After they have proved their faith, God will reward them with life forever. God promised this to all those who love him. ¹³When people are tempted, they should not say, "God is tempting me." Evil cannot tempt God, and God himself does not tempt anyone. ¹⁴But people are tempted when their own evil desire leads them away and traps them. ¹⁵This desire leads to sin, and then the sin grows and brings death.

¹⁶My dear brothers and sisters, do not be fooled about this. ¹⁷Every good action and every perfect gift is from God. These good gifts come down from the Creator of the sun, moon, and stars, who does not change like their shifting shadows. ¹⁸God decided to give us life through the word of truth so we might be the most important of all the things he made.

NKJV

¹²Blessed is the man who endures temptation; for when he has been approved, he will receive the crown of life which the Lord has promised to those who love Him. ¹³Let no one say when he is tempted, "I am tempted by God"; for God cannot be tempted by evil, nor does He Himself tempt anyone. ¹⁴But each one is tempted when he is drawn away by his own desires and enticed. ¹⁵Then, when desire has conceived, it gives birth to sin; and sin, when it is full-grown, brings forth death.

¹⁶Do not be deceived, my beloved brethren. ¹⁷Every good gift and every perfect gift is from above, and comes down from the Father of lights, with whom there is no variation or shadow of turning. ¹⁸Of His own will He brought us forth by the word of truth, that we might be a kind of firstfruits of His creatures.

EXPLORATION

1. How can we remain strong to resist temptation?

2. How does God reward faithful people?

3. Why is it tempting for some people to blame God as the source of temptation?

4. How does James explain the source of our temptations?

5. List the results of continually giving in to sin.

INSPIRATION

The small population of people who saw me play school athletics have never questioned my decision to enter the ministry. I have, however, received a letter reminding me of the time I deep-snapped a football over the punter's head. Another former classmate reminisced with me about the fly ball that slipped out of my glove and allowed the winning run to score. And then there was the time my buddy scored a touchdown on an eighty-yard punt return only to have it called back because his buddy, yours truly, got penalized for clipping. Oh the pain of such memories. They hurt, not just because I messed up, but because I helped the other team. It's bad to lose; it's worse still to help your opponent win!

My most blatant experience of aiding the opposition occurred in a sixth-grade basketball tournament. I can't remember the exact score when I finally got to play, but I know it was close. I recall a loose ball, a scramble to grab it and complete surprise when my teammate on the bottom of the pile threw it to me. When I saw that no one was between me and the basket, I took off. With the style of an MVP-to-be, I made a lay-up worthy of air-time on ESPN. My surprise at the ease of the basket was surpassed only by my surprise at the silence of the crowd.

No one applauded! Rather than pat me on the back, my team buried their faces in their hands. That's when I realized what I'd done. I'd made a basket on the wrong end of the court—I'd aided the enemy! I'd helped the wrong team. No wonder no one tried to stop me—I was helping their side.

Can you imagine how silly I felt? If you can, then you can imagine how silly Satan must feel. Such is the pattern of the devil's day. Every time he sets out to score one for evil, he ends up scoring a point for good. When he schemes to thwart the kingdom, he always advances it. (From *The Great House of God* by Max Lucado)

REACTION

6. List new insights from this Bible passage about temptation. How does Max's quote offer additional incentive to resist temptation?

7. How has the testimony of other believers helped you in your struggle against sin?

8. How does knowing that God is good and gives good things encourage you to fight against sin in your life?

9. What temptations are most difficult for you to resist? Based on this passage, how should you resist those temptations?

10. Is temptation itself sin? How are these two things related?

11. List some ways you can depend more on God for the strength to overcome sin.

LIFE LESSONS

We can do two things when we meet temptation: run from it or face it. Both actions are forms of resistance. The ones we must face with God's wisdom are often the internal ones (we can't very well run away from those). Temptations of fear, selfishness, etc., need to be resisted with the truth of God's Word. Fleeing from or avoiding external temptations is an excellent tactic. Joseph ran away from Pharaoh's seductive wife. In every temptation we need God's help. We need to ask God what we can learn from a temptation we face, rather than relying on human wisdom and questioning God's motives.

DEVOTION

Father, when we confront temptation, we pray that you would give us strength to resist evil. Thank you for your promise that if we do what is right, eventually truth, justice, and goodness will prevail.

For more Bible passages on temptation, see Matthew 6:13; 26:41; Luke 4:1–2; Romans 8:5–8; 1 Corinthians 10:13; Galatians 6:1; Ephesians 6:11–13; Hebrews 4:15–16.

To complete the book of James during this twelve-part study, read James 1:12–18.

JOURNALING

How has God set me free from sin and temptation?

LIVING
PROOF

MAX
LUCADO

REFLECTION

Godliness is not usually listed on many résumés. The word summarizes spiritual maturity, yet is difficult to clearly define. In extended relationships with other believers, we can usually tell who has made progress in godliness. Think of one person in your circle of relationships who truly exemplifies godliness. How has that person's life been an example to you?

SITUATION

James continued his teaching by challenging his readers in the practical areas of listening and doing. Sometimes we need to be quiet and listen to other people. Sometimes we need to prove that we have heard God's Word and get busy doing it. We can tell that we are listening constructively when God's Word begins to change how we see ourselves and how we see other people. Then true godliness will be seen in our being and doing.

OBSERVATION

Read James 1:19–27 from the NCV or the NKJV.

NCV

¹⁹My dear brothers and sisters, always be willing to listen and slow to speak. Do not become angry easily, ²⁰because anger will not help you live the right kind of life God wants. ²¹So put out of your life every evil thing and every kind of wrong. Then in gentleness accept God's teaching that is planted in your hearts, which can save you.

²²Do what God's teaching says; when you only listen and do nothing, you are fooling yourselves. ²³Those who hear God's teaching and do nothing are like people who look at themselves in a mirror. ²⁴They see their faces and then go away and quickly forget what they looked like. ²⁵But the truly happy people are those who carefully study God's perfect law that makes people free, and they continue to study it. They do not forget what they heard, but they obey what God's teaching says. Those who do this will be made happy.

²⁶People who think they are religious but say things they should not say are just fooling themselves. Their "religion" is worth nothing. ²⁷Religion that God accepts as pure and without fault is this: caring for orphans or widows who need help, and keeping yourself free from the world's evil influence.

NKJV

¹⁹So then, my beloved brethren, let every man be swift to hear, slow to speak, slow to wrath; ²⁰for the wrath of man does not produce the righteousness of God.

²¹Therefore lay aside all filthiness and overflow of wickedness, and receive with meekness the implanted word, which is able to save your souls.

²²But be doers of the word, and not hearers only, deceiving yourselves. ²³For if anyone is a hearer of the word and not a doer, he is like a man observing his natural face in a mirror; ²⁴for he observes himself, goes away, and immediately forgets what kind of man he was. ²⁵But he who looks into the perfect law of liberty and continues in it, and is not a forgetful hearer but a doer of the work, this one will be blessed in what he does.

²⁶If anyone among you thinks he is religious, and does not bridle his tongue but deceives his own heart, this one's religion is useless. ²⁷Pure and undefiled religion before God and the Father is this: to visit orphans and widows in their trouble, and to keep oneself unspotted from the world.

EXPLORATION

1. How does this passage describe living a good or godly life? Where does anger fit in?

2. List some of the ways people can deceive themselves.

3. How does this passage describe people who do not obey God's Word?

4. How does God bless those who study and obey his Word's/teaching?

5. How can you practice "pure and undefiled religion"?

INSPIRATION

I'd like to tell you the story of the dancers who had no music. Can you imagine how hard that would be? Dancing with no music? Day after day they came to the great hall just off the corner of Main and Broadway. They brought their wives. They brought their husbands. They brought their children and their hopes. They came to dance.

The hall was prepared for a dance. Streamers strung, punch bowls filled. Chairs were placed against the walls. People arrived and sat, knowing they had come to a dance but not knowing how to dance because they had no music. They had balloons; they had cake. They even had a stage on which the musicians could play, but they had no musicians.

One time a lanky fellow claimed to be a musician. He sure looked the part, what with his belly-length beard and fancy violin. He stood before them and pulled the violin out of the case and placed it beneath his chin. *Now we will dance*, they thought, but they were wrong. For though he had a violin, his violin had no strings. The pushing and pulling of his bow sounded like the creaking of an unoiled door. Who can dance to a sound like that? So the dancers took their seats again . . .

Some tried to dance without the music. One wife convinced her husband to give it a try, so out on the floor they stepped, she dancing her way and he dancing his. A few tried to follow their cue, but since there was no cue, they didn't know how to follow. The result was a dozen or so dancers with no music, going this way and that, bumping into each other and causing more than one observer to seek safety behind a chair.

Those dancers grew weary, and everyone resumed the task of sitting and staring and wondering if anything was ever going to happen. And then one day it did.

Not everyone saw him enter. Only a few. Nothing about his appearance would compel your attention. His looks were common, but his music was not. He began to sing a song, soft and sweet, kind and compelling. His song took the chill out of the air and brought a summer-sunset glow to the heart.

And as he sang, people stood—a few at first, then many—and they began to dance. Together. Flowing to a music they had never heard before, they danced. Some, however, remained seated. What kind of musician is this who never mounts the stage? Who brings no band? Who has no costume? Why, musicians don't just walk in off the street. They have an entourage, a reputation, a persona to project and protect. Why, this fellow scarcely mentioned his name!

"How can we know what you sing is actually music?" they challenged His reply was to the point: "Let the man who has ears to hear use them."

But the nondancers refused to hear. So they refused to dance. Many still refuse. The musician comes and sings. Some dance. Some don't. Some find music for life; others live in silence. To those who miss the music, the musician gives the same appeal: "Let the man who has ears to hear use them." (From *Just Like Jesus Devotional* by Max Lucado)

REACTION

6. How can you have "ears to hear" God's Word this week, and then do it?

7. What pressures does our culture put on us to disobey or disregard God's Word?

8. List some practical ways to protect yourself from the world's influence.

9. In what ways has your life changed since your conversion?

10. Why do we sometimes find it difficult to listen to the Word and do what we know is right?

II. In what ways does your life demonstrate to others that you are a Christian?

LIFE LESSONS

The good news of the gospel of Christ affects the whole person. It's not a set of rules to outwardly follow, but a change deep within that leads to a difference in our behavior. The effects of the gospel in our lives can be seen by a continual process of inward transformation and then outward action that honors God. God's Word frees us to live in truth, and his Spirit gives us the power to live it out.

DEVOTION

Father, help us to hear your voice amid the manifold voices of the world. Help us to put into practice the timeless truths found in your Word. Most of all, Father, help us remember that you have set us free—free from the lures of this world. Thank you for your promise that when the Son sets us free, we are free indeed.

For more Bible passages on obedience, see Leviticus 19:2; Acts 5:29; Romans 6; 2 Corinthians 7:1; 9:13; Titus 3:1; Hebrews 12:13–14; 1 Peter 1:14; 1 John 3:24; 2 John 1:6.

To complete the book of James during this twelve-part study, read James 1:19–27.

JOURNALING

How has God helped me "hear" his Word recently and then obey it?

LESSON FOUR

EQUALITY IN
THE CHURCH

MAX
LUCADO

REFLECTION

Look around and you'll see that it's human nature to revere the wealthy and look down on the poor. Part of being doers of the Word is going against "nature" and not treating people with favoritism, especially in the church. Reflect on a time when you attended a church as a visitor, and think about the positive and negative parts of that experience. When people visit your church, how do you make them feel welcome?

SITUATION

In the atmosphere of social ostracism that existed around the early church, Christians were strongly tempted to treat any prestigious visitors with special deference. The wealthy were given special privileges not extended to other guests. James was determined to confront this partiality that threatened to undermine the gospel and socially fragment the church. The antidote? God's royal law of love.

OBSERVATION

Read James 2:1–13 from the NCV or the NKJV.

NCV

¹My dear brothers and sisters, as believers in our glorious Lord Jesus Christ, never think some people are more important than others. ²Suppose someone comes into your church meeting wearing nice clothes and a gold ring. At the same time a poor person comes in wearing old, dirty clothes. ³You show special attention to the one wearing nice clothes and say, "Please, sit here in this good seat." But you say to the poor person, "Stand over there," or, "Sit on the floor by my feet." ⁴What are you doing? You are making some people more important than others, and with evil thoughts you are deciding that one person is better.

⁵Listen, my dear brothers and sisters! God chose the poor in the world to be rich with faith and to receive the kingdom God promised to those who love him. ⁶But you show no respect to the poor. The rich are always trying to control your lives. They are the ones who take you to court. ⁷And they are the ones who speak against Jesus, who owns you.

⁸This royal law is found in the Scriptures: "Love your neighbor as you love yourself." If you obey this law, you are doing right. ⁹But if you treat one person as being more important than another, you are sinning. You are guilty of breaking God's law. ¹⁰A person who follows all of God's law but fails to obey even one command is guilty of breaking all the commands in that law. ¹¹The same God who said, "You must not be guilty of adultery," also said, "You must not murder anyone." So if you do not take part in adultery but you murder someone, you are guilty of breaking all of God's law. ¹²In everything you say and do, remember that you will be judged by the law that makes people free. ¹³So you must show mercy to others, or God will not show mercy to you when he judges you. But the person who shows mercy can stand without fear at the judgment.

NKJV

¹My brethren, do not hold the faith of our Lord Jesus Christ, the Lord of glory, with partiality. ²For if there should come into your assembly a man with gold rings, in fine apparel, and there should also come in a poor man in filthy clothes, ³and you pay attention to the one wearing the fine clothes and say to him, "You sit here in a good place," and say to the poor man, "You stand there," or, "Sit here at my footstool," ⁴have you not shown partiality among yourselves, and become judges with evil thoughts?

⁵Listen, my beloved brethren: Has God not chosen the poor of this world to be rich in faith and heirs of the kingdom which He promised to those who love Him? ⁶But you have dishonored the poor man. Do not the rich oppress you and drag you into the courts? ⁷Do they not blaspheme that noble name by which you are called?

⁸If you really fulfill the royal law according to the Scripture, "You shall love your neighbor as yourself," you do well; ⁹but if you show partiality, you commit sin, and are convicted by the law as transgressors. ¹⁰For whoever shall keep the whole law, and yet stumble in one point, he is guilty of all. ¹¹For He who said, "Do not commit adultery," also said, "Do not murder." Now if you do not commit adultery, but you do murder, you have become a transgressor of the law. ¹²So speak and so do as those who will be judged by the law of liberty. ¹³For judgment is without mercy to the one who has shown no mercy. Mercy triumphs over judgment.

EXPLORATION

1. Why is it wrong to treat rich people better than poor people?

2. How does God treat the poor and powerless?

3. Explain how partiality makes us unjust judges.

4. How does showing favoritism indicate a feeling of superiority?

5. List some of the ways Christians can show mercy.

INSPIRATION

Our Savior kneels down and gazes upon the darkest acts of our lives. But rather than recoil in horror, he reaches out in kindness and says, "I can clean that if you want." And from the basin of his grace, he scoops a palm full of mercy and washes away our sin.

But that's not all he does. Because he lives in us, you and I can do the same. Because he has forgiven us, we can forgive others. Because he has a forgiving heart, we can have a forgiving heart. We can have a heart like his.

"If I, your Lord and Teacher, have washed your feet, you also should wash each other's feet. I did this as an example so that you should do as I have done for you" (John 13:14–15 NCV).

Jesus washes our feet for two reasons. The first is to give us mercy; the second is to give us a message, and that message is simply this: Jesus offers unconditional grace; we are to offer unconditional grace. The mercy of Christ preceded our mistakes; our mercy must precede the mistakes of others. Those in the circle of Christ had no doubt of his love; those in our circles should have no doubts about ours.

What does it mean to have a heart like his? It means to kneel as Jesus knelt, touching the grimy parts of the people we are stuck with and washing away their unkindness with kindness. Or as Paul wrote, "Be kind and loving to each other, and forgive each other just as God forgave you in Christ" (Eph. 4:32 NCV).

"But, Max," you are saying, "I've done nothing wrong. I'm not the one who cheated. I'm not the one who lied. I'm not the guilty party here." Perhaps you aren't. But neither was Jesus. Of all the men in that room, only one was worthy of having his feet washed. And he was the one who washed the feet. The one worthy of being served, served others. The genius of Jesus' example is that the burden of bridge-building falls on the strong one, not the weak one. The one who is innocent is the one who makes the gesture.

And you know what happens? More often than not, if the one in the right volunteers to wash the feet of the one in the wrong, both parties get on their knees. Don't we all think we are right? Hence we wash each other's feet.

Please understand. *Relationships don't thrive because the guilty are punished but because the innocent are merciful.* (From *Just Like Jesus* by Max Lucado)

REACTION

6. List examples of favoritism or prejudice you see in the church today. How does this illustrate a lack of mercy?

7. List some people you think might feel uncomfortable in your church.

8. What would happen if Jesus brought some of those people to your church next week?

9. If you have been a victim of favoritism or prejudice, how did it make you feel?

10. How can the law of love help change our attitudes toward the poor and vulnerable?

LIFE LESSONS

This passage allows no wiggle room for ambiguity—favoritism is sin. It's based on prejudice, judging others by false standards. Prejudice and favoritism flourish when we stop looking at people the way God looks at them. This also means that we have stopped seeing *ourselves* as God sees us. We need to ask God to help us identify our prejudices and recognize situations in which we tend to show favoritism. Then we need to actively resist these tendencies, asking others to keep us accountable.

DEVOTION

Thank you, Father, that all people are equal in your eyes. Forgive us for judging people by appearances and accomplishments. Forgive us for favoring the rich and powerful over the poor and weak. O God, change our hearts. Teach us what it means to love our neighbors as ourselves.

For more Bible passages on favoritism, see Exodus 23:2–3; Leviticus 19:15; Proverbs 19:6; 1 Timothy 5:21.

To complete the book of James during this twelve-part study, read James 2:1–13.

JOURNALING

How can I gain victory over the sin of favoritism?

HOW FAITH WORKS

MAX LUCADO

REFLECTION

When several people pool their efforts to meet a crisis, an amazing dynamic seems to take over. Perhaps the benefits of working together are almost as great as the benefits of helping someone. Think of a time when you saw a group of people rally around someone in need. What motivated the group to help that person? Were they Christians or not?

SITUATION

Remember that James was writing to believers who were "scattered everywhere in the world" (1:1 NCV). This being the case, James addressed broader issues of faith that were not culture-bound or place-bound. In his blunt, straightforward way, James minced no words when it came to faith and works. Using some heavy-duty Old Testament examples, he argued that a life of faith should be active and proactive.

OBSERVATION

Read James 2:14–26 from the NCV or the NKJV.

NCV

14My brothers and sisters, if people say they have faith, but do nothing, their faith is worth nothing. Can faith like that save them? 15A brother or sister in Christ might need clothes or food. 16If you say to that person, "God be with you! I hope you stay warm and get plenty to eat," but you do not give what that person needs, your words are worth nothing. 17In the same way, faith that is alone—that does nothing—is dead.

18Someone might say, "You have faith, but I have deeds." Show me your faith without doing anything, and I will show you my faith by what I do. 19You believe there is one God. Good! But the demons believe that, too, and they tremble with fear.

20You foolish person! Must you be shown that faith that does nothing is worth nothing? 21Abraham, our ancestor, was made right with God by what he did when he offered his son Isaac on the altar. 22So you see that Abraham's faith and the things he did worked together. His faith was made perfect by what he did. 23This shows the full meaning of the Scripture that says: "Abraham believed God, and God accepted Abraham's faith, and that faith made him right with God." And Abraham was called God's friend. 24So you see that people are made right with God by what they do, not by faith only.

25Another example is Rahab, a prostitute, who was made right with God by something she did. She welcomed the spies into her home and helped them escape by a different road. 26Just as a person's body that does not have a spirit is dead, so faith that does nothing is dead!

NKJV

14What does it profit, my brethren, if someone says he has faith but does not have works? Can faith save him? 15If a brother or sister is naked and destitute of daily food, 16and one of you says to them, "Depart in peace, be warmed and filled," but you do not give them the things which are needed for the body, what does it profit? 17Thus also faith by itself, if it does not have works, is dead.

18But someone will say, "You have faith, and I have works." Show me your faith without your works, and I will show you my faith by my works. 19You believe that there is one God. You do well. Even the demons believe—and tremble! 20But do you want to know, O foolish man, that faith without works is dead? 21Was not Abraham our father justified by works when he offered Isaac his son on the altar? 22Do you see that faith was working together with his works, and by works faith was made perfect? 23And the Scripture was fulfilled which says, "Abraham believed God, and it was accounted to him for righteousness." And he was called the friend of God. 24You see then that a man is justified by works, and not by faith only.

25Likewise, was not Rahab the harlot also justified by works when she received the messengers and sent them out another way?

26For as the body without the spirit is dead, so faith without works is dead also.

EXPLORATION

1. Why is faith without works dead?

2. How is living faith demonstrated?

3. How do some people rationalize inactive faith?

4. Explain why mere belief in God is not enough.

5. How did Abraham and Rahab demonstrate their faith?

INSPIRATION

You and I have the privilege to do for others . . . what God does for us. How do we show people that we believe in them?

Show up. Nothing takes the place of your presence. Letters are nice. Phone calls are special, but being there in the flesh sends a message . . . Do you believe in your kids? Then show up. Show up at their games. Show up at their plays. Show up at their recitals. It may not be possible to make each one, but it's sure worth the effort. An elder in our church supports me with his presence. Whenever I speak at an area congregation, he'll show up. Does nothing. Says little. Just takes a seat in a pew and smiles when we make eye contact. It means a lot to me. In fact, as I write the final draft of this book, he is one room away. Made the ninety-minute drive from his house to my hideout just to pray for me. Do you believe in your friends? Then show up. Show up at their graduations and weddings. Spend time with them. You want to bring out the best in someone? Then show up.

Listen up. You don't have to speak to encourage. The Bible says, "It is best to listen much, speak little" (James 1:19 TLB). We tend to speak much and listen little. There is a time to speak. But there is also a time to be quiet. That's what my father did. Dropping a fly ball may not be a big deal to most people, but if you are thirteen years old and have aspirations of the big leagues, it is a big deal. Not only was it my second error of the game, it allowed the winning run to score. I didn't even go back to the dugout. I turned around in the middle of left field and climbed over the fence. I was halfway home when my dad found me. He didn't say a word. Just pulled over to the side of the road, leaned across the seat, and opened the passenger door. We didn't speak. We didn't need to. We both knew the world had come to an end. When we got home, I went straight to my room, and he went straight to the kitchen. Presently he appeared in front of me with cookies and milk . . . Dad never said a word. But he did show up.

Speak up. Nathaniel Hawthorne came home heartbroken. He'd just been fired from his job in the custom house. His wife, rather than responding with anxiety, surprised him with joy. "Now you can write your book!" He wasn't so positive. "And what shall we live on while I'm writing it?" To his amazement she opened a drawer and revealed a wad of currency she'd saved out of her housekeeping budget. "I always knew you were a man of genius," she told him. "I always knew you'd write a masterpiece." She believed in her husband. And because she did, he wrote. And because he wrote, every library in America has a copy of *The Scarlet Letter* by Nathaniel Hawthorne.

You have the power to change someone's life simply by the words that you speak. "Death and life are in the power of the tongue" (Prov. 18:21 KJV). (From *A Love Worth Giving* by Max Lucado)

REACTION

6. What steps can you take to "show up" and practice true Christianity, through your words and other ways?

7. Why is it important to help others?

8. How is helping others part of a disciplined spiritual life?

9. List ways you can reach out to someone in need in your immediate circumstances.

10. How does spiritual discipline help us to practice true Christianity?

11. How can you develop spiritual discipline in your life?

LIFE LESSONS

The Bible describes faith as belief that results in a dynamic, active response to God's grace. The belief and trust part focuses on God, and the active part focuses on gratitude and obedience. Faith is not "belief in works" or even "belief in faith," but it is works coming out of a settled trust in God. Both workless faith and faithless work fall short. Authentic faith trusts and obeys.

DEVOTION

Father, thank you for your perfect plan of salvation. Thank you for providing a way for us to spend eternity with you. Until then, show us the good work you want us to do and give us the strength to do it.

For more Bible passages on faith and works, see John 14:12; Philippians 2:17; 2 Thessalonians 1:11; Hebrews 6:9−12; 2 Peter 1:5−7.

To complete the book of James during this twelve-part study, read James 2:14−26.

JOURNALING

How do faith and works go together in my life?

TAMING THE
TONGUE

MAX
LUCADO

REFLECTION

A pinch of salt, a pebble in a shoe, and a nail in a tire are all small items that can have large consequences. Think of some other examples of this principle. What are some tiny objects that wield great power or influence?

SITUATION

For James, talk was cheap. Empty claims to faith that didn't result in observable change and action didn't impress him. And yet he appreciated the awesome power of the human speech apparatus. Baseless claims of faith created one kind of danger, but James was also concerned about the destructiveness of out-of-control speech. The tiny tongue could be fire, poison, and evil.

OBSERVATION

Read James 3:1–12 from the NCV or the NKJV.

NCV

¹*My brothers and sisters, not many of you should become teachers, because you know that we who teach will be judged more strictly.* ²*We all make many mistakes. If people never said anything wrong, they would be perfect and able to control their entire selves, too.* ³*When we put bits into the mouths of horses to make them obey us, we can control their whole bodies.* ⁴*Also a ship is very big, and it is pushed by strong winds. But a very small rudder controls that big ship, making it go wherever the pilot wants.* ⁵*It is the same with the tongue. It is a small part of the body, but it brags about great things.*

A big forest fire can be started with only a little flame. ⁶*And the tongue is like a fire. It is a whole world of evil among the parts of our bodies. The tongue spreads its evil through the whole body. The tongue is set on fire by hell, and it starts a fire that influences all of life.* ⁷*People can tame every kind of wild animal, bird, reptile, and fish, and they have tamed them,* ⁸*but no one can tame the tongue. It is wild and evil and full of deadly poison.* ⁹*We use our tongues to praise our Lord and Father, but then we curse people, whom God made like himself.* ¹⁰*Praises and curses come from the same mouth! My brothers and sisters, this should not happen.* ¹¹*Do good and bad water flow from the same spring?* ¹²*My brothers and sisters, can a fig tree make olives, or can a grapevine make figs? No! And a well full of salty water cannot give good water.*

NKJV

¹*My brethren, let not many of you become teachers, knowing that we shall receive a stricter judgment.* ²*For we all stumble in many things. If anyone does not stumble in word, he is a perfect man, able also to bridle the whole body.* ³*Indeed, we put bits in horses' mouths that they may obey us, and we turn their whole body.* ⁴*Look also at ships: although they are so large and are driven by fierce winds, they are turned by a very small rudder wherever the pilot desires.* ⁵*Even so the tongue is a little member and boasts great things.*

See how great a forest a little fire kindles! ⁶*And the tongue is a fire, a world of iniquity. The tongue is so set among our members that it defiles the whole body, and sets on fire the course of nature; and it is set on fire by hell.* ⁷*For every kind of beast and bird, of reptile and creature of the sea, is tamed and has been tamed by mankind.* ⁸*But no man can tame the tongue. It is an unruly evil, full of deadly poison.* ⁹*With it we bless our God and Father, and with it we curse men, who have been made in the similitude of God.* ¹⁰*Out of the same mouth proceed blessing and cursing. My brethren, these things ought not to be so.* ¹¹*Does a spring send forth fresh water and bitter from the same opening?* ¹²*Can a fig tree, my brethren, bear olives, or a grapevine bear figs? Thus no spring yields both salt water and fresh.*

EXPLORATION

1. How does a person's tongue compare to a horse's bit and a ship's rudder?

2. In what ways is the tongue like fire?

3. Explain how the tongue can be used for both good and evil.

4. Why is the tongue so difficult to control? (Realize that something that can't be completely tamed may still yield to determined control.)

5. List the examples from nature that James uses to teach on the power of words.

INSPIRATION

"Whatever you do, do all to the glory of God" (1 Cor. 10:31 NKJV).

Whatever? Whatever.

Let your message reflect his glory. "Let your light shine before men, that they may see your good deeds and praise your Father in heaven" (Matt. 5:16 NIV).

Let your salvation reflect God's glory. "Having believed, you were marked in him with a seal, the promised Holy Spirit, who is a deposit guaranteeing our inheritance until the redemption of those who are God's possession—to the praise of his glory" (Eph. 1:13–14 NIV).

Let your body reflect his glory. "You are not your own . . . Glorify God in your body" (1 Cor. 6:19–20 NKJV).

Your struggles. "These sufferings of ours are for your benefit. And the more of you who are won to Christ, the more there are to thank him for his great kindness, and the more the Lord is glorified" (2 Cor. 4:15 TLB; see also John 11:4).

Your success honors God. "Honor the LORD with your wealth" (Prov. 3:9 NIV). "Riches and honor come from you" (1 Chron. 29:12 NCV). "God . . . is giving you power to make wealth" (Deut. 8:18 NASB).

Your message, your salvation, your body, your struggles, your success—all proclaim God's glory.

"Whatever you do in word or deed, do all in the name of the Lord Jesus, giving thanks through Him to God the Father" (Col. 3:17 NASB).

He's the source; we are the glass. He's the light; we are the mirrors. He sends the message; we mirror it. We rest in his pack awaiting his call. And when placed in his hands, we do his work. It's not about us; it's all about him. (From *It's Not About Me* by Max Lucado)

REACTION

6. How can controlling our tongues bring glory to God? How can our tongues hinder or detract from God's glory?

7. What are some examples of the poison of an untamed tongue?

8. Give some examples of ways our words can encourage others.

9. How can we submit our tongues to the control of God's Spirit?

10. What other Scriptures can you think of that will help you remember to speak encouraging words?

11. To whom can you speak words of blessing today?

LIFE LESSONS

In the big picture of faith and works, James says our speech is the number one indicator of what we believe. How would others describe the color and content of our words? James doesn't want us to convey mixed messages. If the way we speak turns people away, then our faith in action may never get a chance to touch their lives. Is what I'm saying true? Is it necessary? Will it honor God? We need to look at the big picture and not our immediate reactions.

DEVOTION

Father, change us from the inside out. Purify our hearts so that our speech will be pleasing to you. Keep us from using our words to manipulate and hurt others. Empower us by your Holy Spirit to use our tongues to sing your praises and to build others up in the faith.

For more Bible passages on controlling the tongue, see Psalm 34:13; Proverbs 13:3; 21:23; Titus 3:2; James 1:26; 1 Peter 3:10.

To complete the book of James during this twelve-part study, read James 3:1–12.

JOURNALING

What can I do to let God control the words I say?

SOWING
SEEDS OF
PEACE

MAX
LUCADO

REFLECTION

In the middle of conflict, some people use a soothing tone of voice. Some speak firmly while never raising their voices. Others wait patiently until all the verbal heat is spent before they respond. Think of a time when you saw someone bring peace to a volatile situation or light to a dark place. How did that person accomplish it?

SITUATION

Throughout the letter of James there are allusions to the words and wisdom of Jesus. James was Jesus' half brother. Though he did not believe in Jesus before the Resurrection, he did remember much of what Jesus said. This passage on peacemaking echoes the Sermon on the Mount and Jesus' blessing for the peacemakers, for "they shall be called the children of God" (Matt. 5:9 KJV).

OBSERVATION

Read James 3:13—18 from the NCV or the NKJV.

NCV

¹³*Are there those among you who are truly wise and understanding? Then they should show it by living right and doing good things with a gentleness that comes from wisdom.* ¹⁴*But if you are selfish and have bitter jealousy in your hearts, do not brag. Your bragging is a lie that hides the truth.* ¹⁵*That kind of "wisdom" does not come from God but from the world. It is not spiritual; it is from the devil.* ¹⁶*Where jealousy and selfishness are, there will be confusion and every kind of evil.* ¹⁷*But the wisdom that comes from God is first of all pure, then peaceful, gentle, and easy to please. This wisdom is always ready to help those who are troubled and to do good for others. It is always fair and honest.* ¹⁸*People who work for peace in a peaceful way plant a good crop of right-living.*

NKJV

¹³*Who is wise and understanding among you? Let him show by good conduct that his works are done in the meekness of wisdom.* ¹⁴*But if you have bitter envy and self-seeking in your hearts, do not boast and lie against the truth.* ¹⁵*This wisdom does not descend from above, but is earthly, sensual, demonic.* ¹⁶*For where envy and self-seeking exist, confusion and every evil thing are there.* ¹⁷*But the wisdom that is from above is first pure, then peaceable, gentle, willing to yield, full of mercy and good fruits, without partiality and without hypocrisy.* ¹⁸*Now the fruit of righteousness is sown in peace by those who make peace.*

EXPLORATION

1. How would you describe "worldly wisdom"?

2. How does Scripture describe God's wisdom?

3. Why do jealousy and selfishness cause confusion and evil things?

4. What happens when people work for peace?

INSPIRATION

"Those who are peacemakers will plant seeds of peace and reap a harvest of goodness" (James 3:18 TLB). The principle for peace is the same as the principle for crops: Never underestimate the power of a seed.

The story of Heinz is a good example. Europe, 1934. Hitler's plague of anti-Semitism was infecting a continent. Some would escape it. Some would die from it. But eleven-year-old Heinz would learn from it. He would learn the power of sowing seeds of peace.

Heinz was a Jew. The Bavarian village of Furth where Heinz lived was being overrun by Hitler's young thugs. Heinz's father, a schoolteacher, lost his job. Recreational activities ceased . . . Hitler youth roamed the neighborhoods looking for trouble. Young Heinz learned to keep his eyes open. When he saw a band of troublemakers, he would step to the other side of the street. Sometimes he would escape a fight—sometimes not.

One day, in 1934, a pivotal confrontation occurred. Heinz found himself face-to-face with a Hitler bully. A beating appeared inevitable. This time, however, he walked away unhurt—not because of what he did, but because of what he said. He didn't fight back; he spoke up. He convinced the troublemakers that a fight was not necessary. His words kept battle at bay. And Heinz saw firsthand how the tongue can create peace. He learned the skill of using words to avoid conflict. And for a young Jew in Hitler-ridden Europe, that skill had many opportunities to be honed.

Fortunately, Heinz's family escaped from Bavaria and made their way to America. Later in life, he would downplay the impact those adolescent experiences had on his development. But one has to wonder. For after Heinz grew up, his name became synonymous with peace negotiations. His legacy became that of a bridge builder. Somewhere he had learned the power of the properly placed word of peace. You don't know him as Heinz. You know him by his Anglicized name, *Henry*. Henry Kissinger.

Never underestimate the power of a seed. (From *The Applause of Heaven* by Max Lucado)

REACTION

5. How does a wise person resolve conflict?

6. What do you think it means to sow seeds of peace?

7. Why are people sometimes unwilling to work for peace?

8. How does this passage challenge you to deal with conflicts in your relationships?

9. Why is it important for Christians to sow seeds of peace?

10. List some practical ways you can bring peace to a conflict you are facing.

BOOK OF JAMES

LIFE LESSONS

When we face conflict that is escalating, hit the "pause" button and think it through. If envy, anger, or selfish ambition is present, wisdom is usually absent. Before we speak or engage in a conflict situation, it's wise to run our plans past the eight traits of wisdom that James listed. Is what I'm about to propose pure, peaceable, gentle, submissive, merciful, fruitful, impartial, and sincere? If our thoughts don't pass these tests, it's time to rethink.

DEVOTION

Father, we don't always want to seek peace. Forgive us. Keep us from contributing to conflict instead of resolving it, for fanning flames of discord instead of spreading peace. Give us your wisdom, Father—wisdom to be submissive, merciful, and gentle.

For more Bible passages on wisdom and peace, see Psalms 29:11; 34:14; 119:165; Proverbs 2:6; 3:13; 4:7; Daniel 12:3; John 14:27; Romans 8:6; Philippians 4:7; Colossians 2:2–3.

To complete the book of James during this twelve-part study, read James 3:13–18.

JOURNALING

How can I bring peace to conflict at home, work, school, or church?

LESSON EIGHT

TRUSTING
GOD

REFLECTION

According to James, we can live for God—giving up our rights and trusting him to provide; or we can live like the world—claiming our rights. Too often there is just as much selfish bickering going on in the church as in the world. When was the last time you humbled yourself and admitted you were wrong about something?

SITUATION

Despite his previous words about godly wisdom and peacemaking, James seemed to sense that handling conflicts within the church needed more attention. He wanted his readers to understand that part of peacemaking involves a grasp on the underlying causes of conflicts. He laid bare the human tendency toward self-ishness and insisted that the answer must be submission to God.

OBSERVATION

Read James 4:1–10 from the NCV or the NKJV.

NCV

¹Do you know where your fights and arguments come from? They come from the selfish desires that war within you. ²You want things, but you do not have them. So you are ready to kill and are jealous of other people, but you still cannot get what you want. So you argue and fight. You do not get what you want, because you do not ask God. ³Or when you ask, you do not receive because the reason you ask is wrong. You want things so you can use them for your own pleasures.

⁴So, you are not loyal to God! You should know that loving the world is the same as hating God. Anyone who wants to be a friend of the world becomes God's enemy. ⁵Do you think the Scripture means nothing that says, "The Spirit that God made to live in us wants us for himself alone." ⁶But God gives us even more grace, as the Scripture says,

"God is against the proud,

but he gives grace to the humble."

⁷So give yourselves completely to God. Stand against the devil, and the devil will run from you. ⁸Come near to God, and God will come near to you. You sinners, clean sin out of your lives. You who are trying to follow God and the world at the same time, make your thinking pure. ⁹Be sad, cry, and weep! Change your laughter into crying and your joy into sadness. ¹⁰Don't be too proud in the Lord's presence, and he will make you great.

NKJV

¹Where do wars and fights come from among you? Do they not come from your desires for pleasure that war in your members? ²You lust and do not have. You murder and covet and cannot obtain. You fight and war. Yet you do not have because you do not ask. ³You ask and do not receive, because you ask amiss, that you may spend it on your pleasures. ⁴Adulterers and adulteresses! Do you not know that friendship with the world is enmity with God? Whoever therefore wants to be a friend of the world makes himself an enemy of God. ⁵Or do you think that the Scripture says in vain, "The Spirit who dwells in us yearns jealously"?

⁶But He gives more grace. Therefore He says:

"God resists the proud,

But gives grace to the humble."

⁷Therefore submit to God. Resist the devil and he will flee from you. ⁸Draw near to God and He will draw near to you. Cleanse your hands, you sinners; and purify your hearts, you double-minded. ⁹Lament and mourn and weep! Let your laughter be turned to mourning and your joy to gloom. ¹⁰Humble yourselves in the sight of the Lord, and He will lift you up.

EXPLORATION

1. What causes the "wars" within us and around us in our relationships?

2. What does it mean to be a "friend of the world"?

3. List some of the ways we can stand against the devil (vv. 7–9).

4. What promise is given to those who draw near to God?

5. What are we to lament and mourn over?

INSPIRATION

David rejoiced to say, "The LORD is my shepherd," and in so doing he proudly implied, "I am his sheep."

Still uncomfortable with being considered a sheep? Will you humor me and take a simple quiz? See if you succeed in self-reliance. Raise your hand if any of the following describe you.

You can control your moods. You're never grumpy or sullen. You can't relate to Jekyll and Hyde. You're always upbeat and upright. Does that describe you? No? Well, let's try another.

You're at peace with everyone. Every relationship as sweet as fudge. Even your old flames speak highly of you. Love all and are loved by all. Is that you? If not, how about this description?

You have no fears. Call you the Teflon toughie. Wall Street plummets—no problem. Heart condition discovered—yawn. World War III starts—what's for dinner? Does this describe you?

You need no forgiveness. Never made a mistake. As square as a game of checkers. As clean as grandma's kitchen. Never cheated, never lied, never lied about cheating. Is that you? No?

Let's evaluate this. You can't control your moods. A few of your relationships are shaky. You have fears and faults. Hmmm. Do you really want to hang on to your chest of self-reliance? Sounds to me as if you could use a shepherd. Otherwise, you might end up with a Twenty-third Psalm like this:

I am my own shepherd, I am always in need.

I stumble from mall to mall and shrink to shrink, seeking relief but never finding it.

I creep through the valley of the shadow of death and fall apart.

I fear everything from pesticides to power lines, and I'm starting to act like my mother.

I go down to the weekly staff meeting and am surrounded by enemies. I go home, and even the goldfish scowls at me.

I anoint my headache with extra-strength Tylenol.

My Jack Daniel's runneth over.

Surely misery and misfortune will follow me, and I will live in self-doubt for the rest of my lonely life.

Why is it that the ones who most need a shepherd resist him so? (From *Traveling Light* by Max Lucado)

REACTION

6. Why do we resist relying on and submitting to God?

7. How can humbling ourselves before God affect our other relationships?

8. When have you been convinced that you knew God's will for you? What convinced you?

9. List areas of your life that are difficult for you to turn over to God's control.

10. What truth in this lesson encourages you to trust God more fully?

11. What steps can you take to draw nearer to God?

LIFE LESSONS

Who do you want to please? The choice is simple, yet hard. We can please God or someone else (including ourselves). We were created for God's pleasure and glory, but we will sink into petty selfish behavior if we don't humbly bow before God. We can choose friendship with God or friendship with the world (including ourselves). As James shows us in the passage, we can troubleshoot almost any problem we get into by asking, "Who am I trying to please?"

DEVOTION

Father, help us renew our commitment to you—to release all that we have and all that we are to you. We long to give ourselves completely to you so that we might know the freedom available to us only through your grace.

For more Bible passages on trusting God, see Psalms 62:8; 143:8; Proverbs 29:25; Isaiah 25:9; Nahum 1:7; Romans 10:11.

To complete the book of James during this twelve-part study, read James 4:1–10.

JOURNALING

How am I living my life to demonstrate my trust in God?

LESSON NINE

THE DANGERS
OF PRIDE

MAX
LUCADO

REFLECTION

"No one plans to fail, but many fail to plan," goes the saying. Planning is big in our culture. We set our goals, and we feel pretty good when we reach them. We are in control when we make our plans happen, right? What is one of your long-range goals? How would you feel if you could not accomplish it?

SITUATION

James discussed faith and works, the sins of the tongue, and the peaceful wisdom from God. But there is still trouble in the church because of the P word: pride. Apparently there was some gossiping and lying and judging going on; James dealt with it bluntly. He also warned them to remember that all our tomorrows, like everything else, come to us from God's gracious hand.

OBSERVATION

Read James 4:11–17 from the NCV or the NKJV.

NCV

11Brothers and sisters, do not tell evil lies about each other. If you speak against your fellow believers or judge them, you are judging and speaking against the law they follow. And when you are judging the law, you are no longer a follower of the law. You have become a judge. 12God is the only Lawmaker and Judge. He is the only One who can save and destroy. So it is not right for you to judge your neighbor.

13Some of you say, "Today or tomorrow we will go to some city. We will stay there a year, do business, and make money." 14But you do not know what will happen tomorrow! Your life is like a mist. You can see it for a short time, but then it goes away. 15So you should say, "If the Lord wants, we will live and do this or that." 16But now you are proud and you brag. All of this bragging is wrong. 17Anyone who knows the right thing to do, but does not do it, is sinning.

NKJV

11Do not speak evil of one another, brethren. He who speaks evil of a brother and judges his brother, speaks evil of the law and judges the law. But if you judge the law, you are not a doer of the law but a judge. 12There is one Lawgiver, who is able to save and to destroy. Who are you to judge another?

13Come now, you who say, "Today or tomorrow we will go to such and such a city, spend a year there, buy and sell, and make a profit"; 14whereas you do not know what will happen tomorrow. For what is your life? It is even a vapor that appears for a little time and then vanishes away. 15Instead you ought to say, "If the Lord wills, we shall live and do this or that." 16But now you boast in your arrogance. All such boasting is evil.

17Therefore, to him who knows to do good and does not do it, to him it is sin.

EXPLORATION

1. According to James, why should we not speak against fellow Christians?

2. In what ways do we judge others and end up judging "the law"?

3. When does planning turn into boastful pride?

4. What attitude does God want us to have about the future? Why?

5. Why is God not satisfied that we simply *know* to do good?

INSPIRATION

A prison of pride is filled with self-made men and women determined to pull themselves up by their own bootstraps even if they land on their rear ends. It doesn't matter what they did or to whom they did it, or where they end up; it only matters that "I did it my way."

You've seen the prisoners. You've seen the alcoholic who won't admit his drinking problem. You've seen the woman who refuses to talk to anyone about her fears. You've seen the businessman who adamantly rejects help, even when his dreams are falling apart.

Perhaps to see such a prisoner all you have to do is look in the mirror.

"If we confess our sins . . ." The biggest word in the Scriptures just might be that two letter one, *if.* For confessing sins—admitting failure—is exactly what prisoners of pride refuse to do.

"Well, I may not be perfect, but I'm better than Hitler and certainly kinder than Idi Amin!"

"Me a sinner? Oh, sure, I get rowdy every so often, but I'm a pretty good ol' boy."

"Listen, I'm just as good as the next guy. I pay my taxes. I coach the Little League team. I even make donations to Red Cross. Why, God's probably proud to have someone like me on his team."

Justification. Rationalization. Comparison. These are the tools of the jailbird. They sound good. They sound familiar. They even sound American. But in the kingdom, they sound hollow . . .

When you get to the point of sorrow for your sins, when you admit that you have no other option but to cast all your cares on him, and when there is truly no other one that you can call, then cast all your cares on him, for he is waiting. (From *The Applause of Heaven* by Max Lucado)

REACTION

6. Why is humility harder to practice than pride?

7. What part does pride play in judging others?

8. Who do you know who demonstrates a spirit of humility? What have you learned from that person?

9. How has pride damaged your relationship with God or others?

10. How can you begin to bring change and healing to those relationships?

11. What steps can you take to develop a spirit of humility as you plan for the future?

LIFE LESSONS

When Jesus told us not to worry about tomorrow (Matt. 6:34), he was not rejecting the importance of planning. In fact worrying about tomorrow is sometimes an indication that we haven't planned enough. James's counsel is to prepare for what we can, always acknowledging God's ultimate control over tomorrow. Trusting him is the best way to keep from being consumed by worry or betrayed by arrogance in assuming that tomorrow will run as we've planned.

DEVOTION

Father, forgive us for living for ourselves, for thinking that we don't need you. God, help us to embrace humility. Help us to remember that we can do nothing without you, because you are the source of everything.

For more Bible passages on pride, see Proverbs 11:2; 13:10; 16:5, 18; Romans 12:16; 1 Peter 5:5.

To complete the book of James during this twelve-part study, read James 4:11–17.

JOURNALING

How am I encouraged to know that God controls my future?

WARNINGS
TO THE RICH

MAX
LUCADO

REFLECTION

Even if we are not wealthy, most of us know someone who is. "The love of money causes all kinds of evil," the Bible says (1 Tim. 6:10 NCV). But it can also be used for good. Think of a time when you were blessed by the financial generosity of a fellow believer. How has the generosity of others affected your life?

SITUATION

Up to this point in the letter, James wrote with all the believers in mind. Then he zeroed in on those who were wealthy, especially crooked employers. They were mentioned earlier as being favored over others by the rest of the church. James boldly targeted the rich with some shocking words about their future plight.

OBSERVATION

Read James 5:1–6 from the NCV or the NKJV.

NCV

¹You rich people, listen! Cry and be very sad because of the troubles that are coming to you. ²Your riches have rotted, and your clothes have been eaten by moths. ³Your gold and silver have rusted, and that rust will be a proof that you were wrong. It will eat your bodies like fire. You saved your treasure for the last days. ⁴The pay you did not give the workers who mowed your fields cries out against you, and the cries of the workers have been heard by the Lord All-Powerful. ⁵Your life on earth was full of rich living and pleasing yourselves with everything you wanted. You made yourselves fat, like an animal ready to be killed. ⁶You have judged guilty and then murdered innocent people, who were not against you.

NKJV

¹Come now, you rich, weep and howl for your miseries that are coming upon you! ²Your riches are corrupted, and your garments are moth-eaten. ³Your gold and silver are corroded, and their corrosion will be a witness against you and will eat your flesh like fire. You have heaped up treasure in the last days. ⁴Indeed the wages of the laborers who mowed your fields, which you kept back by fraud, cry out; and the cries of the reapers have reached the ears of the Lord of Sabaoth. ⁵You have lived on the earth in pleasure and luxury; you have fattened your hearts as in a day of slaughter. ⁶You have condemned, you have murdered the just; he does not resist you.

EXPLORATION

1. In what ways have you seen people oppress others for personal gain?

2. List some ungodly attitudes that cause oppression.

3. How does God respond to the oppressed?

4. What results from self-indulgence?

INSPIRATION

We live at one of the great turning points in history. The present division of the world's resources dares not continue. And it will not. Either courageous pioneers will persuade reluctant nations to share the good earth's bounty, or we will enter an era of catastrophic conflict.

Christians should be in the vanguard. The church of Jesus Christ is the most universal body in the world today. All we need to do is truly obey the One we rightly worship. But to obey will mean to follow. And he lives among the poor and oppressed, seeking justice for those in agony. In our time, following in his steps will mean more simple personal lifestyles. It will mean transformed churches . . . costly commitment to structural change in secular society.

Do Christians today have that kind of faith and courage? Will we pioneer new models of sharing for our interdependent world? Will we dare to become the vanguard in the struggle for structural change? . . . I am not pessimistic. God regularly accomplishes his will through faithful remnants. Even in affluent nations, there are millions of Christians who love their Lord Jesus more than houses and lands. More and more Christians are coming to realize that their Lord calls them to feed the hungry and seek justice for the oppressed.

If at this moment in history a few million Christians in affluent nations dare to join hands with the poor around the world, we will decisively influence the course of world history. Together we will strive to be a biblical people ready to follow wherever Scripture leads. We must pray for the courage to bear any cross, suffer any loss, and joyfully embrace any sacrifice that biblical faith requires in an age of hunger. (From *Rich Christians in an Age of Hunger* by Ronald J. Sider)

REACTION

5. List some of the negative effects that increased wealth can have on people's lives.

6. How can you use your financial resources for God's glory?

7. How can money keep you from doing God's work?

8. In what ways do you need to change your attitudes about money?

9. How can sharing your wealth improve the state of the world?

LIFE LESSONS

Whether or not we consider ourselves among the rich, these words of James can make us feel uncomfortable. They are meant to. Sizable wealth or not, we tend to base our security on it rather than on God. Anxiety over money—keeping it, growing it, protecting it—can drive us far from our only true security in Christ. And when a wealth-centered life affects the way we treat others, we are on our way to spiritual bankruptcy. James's hard words are merciful warnings.

DEVOTION

Father, keep us from being so blinded by earthly possessions that we fail to see the eternal treasure we cannot lose. Forgive us when we have worked for greed and gain. Thank you for the blessing of work and for the strength to do it for you.

For more Bible passages on warnings to the rich, see Proverbs 11:28; 23:4; Matthew 19:23–24; Luke 6:24; 1 Timothy 6:9–10; 17–19.

To complete the book of James during this twelve-part study, read James 5:1–6.

JOURNALING

How content am I with my financial situation?

LESSON ELEVEN

THE
REWARDS OF
PERSEVERANCE

MAX
LUCADO

REFLECTION

The book of James is nothing if not practical. Our faith is to be lived out. So how are you doing? Consider whether you've been able to face a recent trial or temptation with joy. Have you persevered in spite of difficult circumstances? What have been the rewards for your perseverance?

SITUATION

James changed his tone toward the end of his letter and spoke again to his "brothers and sisters," encouraging them to have patience and hope. Jesus will return! James reminded them that other people of faith had endured and made it; so would they. No matter what their present circumstances, they could count on God's compassion and mercy.

OBSERVATION

Read James 5:7–11 from the NCV or the NKJV.

NCV

7Brothers and sisters, be patient until the Lord comes again. A farmer patiently waits for his valuable crop to grow from the earth and for it to receive the autumn and spring rains. 8You, too, must be patient. Do not give up hope, because the Lord is coming soon. 9Brothers and sisters, do not complain against each other or you will be judged guilty. And the Judge is ready to come! 10Brothers and sisters, follow the example of the prophets who spoke for the Lord. They suffered many hard things, but they were patient. 11We say they are happy because they did not give up. You have heard about Job's patience, and you know the Lord's purpose for him in the end. You know the Lord is full of mercy and is kind.

NKJV

7Therefore be patient, brethren, until the coming of the Lord. See how the farmer waits for the precious fruit of the earth, waiting patiently for it until it receives the early and latter rain. 8You also be patient. Establish your hearts, for the coming of the Lord is at hand.

9Do not grumble against one another, brethren, lest you be condemned. Behold, the Judge is standing at the door! 10My brethren, take the prophets, who spoke in the name of the Lord, as an example of suffering and patience. 11Indeed we count them blessed who endure. You have heard of the perseverance of Job and seen the end intended by the Lord—that the Lord is very compassionate and merciful.

EXPLORATION

1. Why should believers be motivated to patiently endure?

2. How does the illustration of a farmer show the importance of patience? Can you think of similar examples?

3. Whose example should believers follow? Why?

4. What did the prophets gain from their suffering?

5. How was God's compassion and mercy extended to Job?

INSPIRATION

Julie Lindsey was working the late shift at a hotel just south of Montgomery, Alabama. Her part-time employment helped pay her college bills as she finished school. She was a devout believer. But her belief was tested the night two men held a gun to her head and forced her into their truck. She was robbed, repeatedly raped, and left handcuffed to a tree. It was two o'clock in the morning before she was rescued.

The nightmare nearly destroyed her. She couldn't function, the hotel fired her, and she dropped out of school. In her words, she was "shattered, lost, and bewildered."

This is one of the pieces that doesn't fit the puzzle. How does such a tragedy have a place in God's plan? In time, Julie learned the answer to that question. Listen to her words:

After this experience, I spent a great deal of time thinking about God . . . I searched and I prayed for understanding. I longed to be healed . . . My spirit and faith were sorely tested, my spiritual journey in the months that followed was painful, but also wonderful. God allowed me to profit from an awful and devastating event. So many good things are in my life now. I have wonderful friends—most of whom I would never have met or known were it not for this experience. I have a job that allows me to work with and serve crime victims. I have a deeper relationship with God. I am spiritually wiser and more mature. I have been blessed beyond what I can tell in these pages, and I am very grateful. Romans 8:28 came alive in my life: "All things work together for good for those who love God and are called according to his purpose."

Now I ask you, who won? Julie now has a ministry speaking to groups about God's mercy and healing. Can't you imagine the devil groaning with each message? What he intended for evil, God used for good. Satan unknowingly advanced the cause of the kingdom. Rather than destroy a disciple, he strengthened a disciple.

Think about that the next time evil flaunts its cape and races across your stage. Remember, the final act has already been scripted. And the day Christ comes will be the end of evil. (From *When Christ Comes* by Max Lucado)

REACTION

6. When has it been difficult for you to persevere in your Christian walk?

7. List some ways that Christian friends have encouraged you to persevere in tough times.

8. How can you pass that along and encourage others to trust God and endure through suffering?

9. How does knowing that Jesus will return give you hope?

10. What new insight about God's character have you gained from this lesson?

11. In what ways have you experienced God's mercy in your life recently?

LIFE LESSONS

Perseverance is an interesting topic of conversation in a Bible study. It takes on a bit more weight in a setting of pressure, crisis, or tragedy. And we will have troubles, James says. It's not easy to persevere when we need to persevere. God offers us the assurance of his presence. He reminds us of saints in his Word who have endured far more than we probably face. And he tells us that no matter what our present circumstances may be, God will have the last word.

DEVOTION

Father, you never promised us that this world would be easy; you never said there would be no pain. But you did promise that if we persevere, we would be blessed by your mercy and your grace. Teach us to hold firmly to your promises, so that we can endure the struggles and storms of this world.

For more Bible passages on perseverance, see Romans 2:7; 5:3–4; 8:24–25; 1 Timothy 4:16; Hebrews 10:36; 12:1; James 1:2–4, 12; 2 Peter 1:5–9.

To complete the book of James during this twelve-part study, read James 5:7–11.

JOURNALING

How can the promise of Christ's return help me face my daily struggles?

LESSON TWELVE

PRAYERS OF
FAITH

MAX
LUCADO

REFLECTION

From time to time, it's helpful to consider our prayer habits. Are we praying with faith, expecting God to act, or just praying out of routine? One way to shake up the routine is to take time to remember what God has done. Think of a time when God answered a specific prayer for you. How did that answered prayer change your life?

SITUATION

James began his letter encouraging his readers to pray for wisdom when they needed it. He ended his letter with a call to pray about all the situations of their lives, knowing that their prayers would accomplish much as they rely on God. He urged them to be real and support one another in community and thus continue the adventure of living out their faith together as the body of Christ.

OBSERVATION

Read James 5:12–20 from the NCV or the NKJV.

NCV

¹²My brothers and sisters, above all, do not use an oath when you make a promise. Don't use the name of heaven, earth, or anything else to prove what you say. When you mean yes, say only yes, and when you mean no, say only no so you will not be judged guilty.

¹³Anyone who is having troubles should pray. Anyone who is happy should sing praises. ¹⁴Anyone who is sick should call the church's elders. They should pray for and pour oil on the person in the name of the Lord. ¹⁵And the prayer that is said with faith will

make the sick person well; the Lord will heal that person. And if the person has sinned,
the sins will be forgiven. ¹⁶Confess your sins to each other and pray for each other so
God can heal you. When a believing person prays, great things happen. ¹⁷Elijah was a
human being just like us. He prayed that it would not rain, and it did not rain on the
land for three and a half years! ¹⁸Then Elijah prayed again, and the rain came down
from the sky, and the land produced crops again.

¹⁹My brothers and sisters, if one of you wanders away from the truth, and someone helps
that person come back, ²⁰remember this: Anyone who brings a sinner back from the
wrong way will save that sinner's soul from death and will cause many sins to be forgiven.

NKJV

¹²But above all, my brethren, do not swear, either by heaven or by earth or with any
other oath. But let your "Yes," be "Yes," and your "No," "No," lest you fall into judgment.

¹³Is anyone among you suffering? Let him pray. Is anyone cheerful? Let him sing psalms.
¹⁴Is anyone among you sick? Let him call for the elders of the church, and let them pray
over him, anointing him with oil in the name of the Lord. ¹⁵And the prayer of faith will
save the sick, and the Lord will raise him up. And if he has committed sins, he will be
forgiven. ¹⁶Confess your trespasses to one another, and pray for one another, that you
may be healed. The effective, fervent prayer of a righteous man avails much. ¹⁷Elijah
was a man with a nature like ours, and he prayed earnestly that it would not rain; and
it did not rain on the land for three years and six months. ¹⁸And he prayed again, and
the heaven gave rain, and the earth produced its fruit.

¹⁹Brethren, if anyone among you wanders from the truth, and someone turns him back,
²⁰let him know that he who turns a sinner from the error of his way will save a soul
from death and cover a multitude of sins.

EXPLORATION

1. Summarize in your own words James's final instruction about the tongue.

2. What advice and comfort did James give to the troubled, the cheerful, and the sick?

3. What steps should believers take to receive God's healing?

4. What kind of prayer makes great things happen? What do the words *effective* and *avails* mean in verse 16?

5. What does Elijah's experience teach believers about prayer?

INSPIRATION

If there ever was a DTP [Destructive Thought Patterns] candidate, it was George. Abandoned by his father, orphaned by his mother, the little boy was shuffled from foster parent to homelessness and back several times. A sitting duck for bitterness and anger, George could have spent his life getting even. But he didn't. He didn't because Mariah Watkins taught him to think good thoughts.

The needs of each attracted the other—Mariah, a childless washer-woman, and George, a homeless orphan. When Mariah discovered the young boy sleeping in her barn, she took him in. Not only that, she took care of him, took him to church, and helped him find his way to God. When George left Mariah's home, among his few possessions was a Bible she'd given him. By the time he left her home, she had left her mark.

And by the time George left this world, he had left his.

George—George Washington Carver—is a father of modern agriculture. History credits him with more than three hundred products extracted from peanuts alone. The once-orphaned houseguest of Mariah Watkins became the friend of Henry Ford, Mahatma Gandhi, and three presidents. He entered his laboratory every morning with the prayer, "Open thou mine eyes, that I may behold wondrous things out of thy law."

God answers such prayers. He changes the man by changing the mind. And how does it happen? By doing what you are doing right now. Considering the glory of Christ. "But we all, with unveiled face, beholding as in a mirror the glory of the Lord, are being transformed into the same image from glory to glory, just as from the Lord, the Spirit" (2 Cor. 3:18 NASB).

To behold him is to become like him. As Christ dominates your thoughts, he changes you from one degree of glory to another until—hang on!—you are ready to live with him.

Heaven is the land of sinless minds. Virus-free thinking. Absolute trust. No fear or anger. Shame and second-guessing are practices of a prior life. Heaven will be wonderful, not because the streets are gold, but because our thoughts will be pure.

So what are you waiting for? Apply God's antivirus. "Set your minds on the things above, not on the things that are on earth" (Col. 3:2 NASB). Give him your best thoughts, and see if he doesn't change your mind. (From *Next Door Savior* by Max Lucado)

REACTION

6. What keeps people from turning to God in prayer?

7. When has it been difficult for you to accept God's answer to your prayer?

8. How can you develop more discipline and patience in your prayer life?

9. What great things would you like to see God do in your life or the lives of others?

10. What commitment are you willing to make to pray for those things?

11. Who can keep you accountable to follow through on your commitment?

LIFE LESSONS

Prayer should be the default setting for a Christian's life. "Pray without ceasing" (1 Thess. 5:17 NKJV), the apostle Paul said, and James would have concurred. What begins as a conscious and deliberate habit can become, over time, a way of living that maintains constant contact with God. The challenges of life and the needs of other people become opportunities to bring to the forefront the prayer life that is going on in the background of our minds continuously. That's the effective prayer life that avails much!

DEVOTION

Father, we cherish your promise to answer our prayers. And yet we often come to you with muddled ideas, unsure of what is best, uncertain of your will, and unwilling to wait patiently for your answers. We thank you, Father, for the assurance that our imperfect prayers cannot hinder your incredible power.

For more Bible passages on prayer, see Psalm 6:9; Proverbs 15:8, 29; Matthew 21:22; Philippians 4:6–7; Colossians 4:2; 1 Peter 3:12.

To complete the book of James during this twelve-part study, read James 5:12–20.

JOURNALING

Write a prayer to God about a situation that is troubling you.